RADICAL DISCIPLESHIP

Radical Discipleship

Consecrated Life and the Call to Holiness

~

Francis Cardinal Arinze

IGNATIUS PRESS   SAN FRANCISCO

Cover art:

Christ and the Rich Young Ruler (detail)
by Heinrich Hofmann (1824–1911)
Riverside Church, New York City
Courtesy of Wikimedia Commons

Cover design by Davin Carlson

© 2015 by Ignatius Press, San Francisco
All rights reserved
ISBN 978-1-62164-010-3
Library of Congress Control Number 2014949950
Printed in the United States of America ∞

Contents

Introduction

Our Lord and Savior Jesus Christ has by his life, example, and teaching attracted millions of people to follow him through the centuries. Indeed, his invitation to his first disciples was "Follow me." The four Evangelists all record this (cf. Mt 4:19; 8:22; 9:9; Mk 1:17; 2:14; Lk 5:27; 9:59; 18:22; Jn 1:43; 21:19, 22). Christianity was in the earliest days called "the Way". The Acts of the Apostles uses this term without further qualification six times (cf. Acts 9:2; 19:9, 23; 22:4; 24:14, 22). Three times there is further specification: "the way of salvation" in Acts 16:17; "the way of the Lord" in Acts 18:25; and "the way of God" in Acts 18:26. The religion established by Jesus Christ is understood as a following of Christ. The Second Vatican Council regards the Church as the people of God, "a messianic people" (*Lumen Gentium*, 9) that walks through history, following Christ. It was later in Antioch that the disciples of Christ "were for the first time called Christians" (Acts 11:26).

One of the most radical ways of following Jesus is what has in the history of the Church developed and been technically called "the consecrated state".

Pope Francis has declared 2015 the Year of Consecrated Life. This little book is an effort to contribute
to reflection on the consecrated life in the Church.
It is not a dissertation based on deep research on the
theology of the consecrated life and the canon law
pertaining to it. There are already many publications
on that. What is offered here is a reflection, with the
hope and prayer that this life may be better understood, loved, lived, and promoted.

We shall first ask ourselves what are the origins of
the consecrated life, starting from the Gospel itself.
The essentials and various forms of this life will next
be examined. An idea will be given of the number of
consecrated men and women in the Church of our
days. The Church has shown in many ways her appreciation of life in the consecrated state, and it is as
well that a little of this be recalled. A central consideration has to be the three evangelical counsels that all
consecrated people take as vows. Community life is
part and parcel of most forms of the consecrated life
and needs our attention. The prophetic dimension
of the consecrated life is striking to all observers, and
we need to thank God for it. Thereafter, the vocation
of religious brothers will be reflected upon because
some people have quite a problem in understanding
and respecting it. The consecrated state brings many
blessings to Church and society, and some of these
need to be recalled. As in all states of life, there are

some consecrated people who do not persevere in that state to the end. An examination of some of the problems and challenges involved in consecrated life can help to encourage many more to persevere in this vocation. This book will close with a consideration of some of the responsibilities of the whole Church toward the consecrated state.

I

Origins of the
Consecrated Life

Our Master Jesus Christ lived a life that was poor,
chaste, and obedient. His followers strive to follow
him, each person according to his vocation and mission. The call to the Christian life is in itself a call
to holiness, which is the perfection of charity. Jesus
himself invited all his followers to be perfect, as their
heavenly Father is perfect (cf. Mt 5:48). He did not
institute the consecrated state in the same way in
which he gave us the sacred priesthood. Nevertheless, his life and his teaching lead to the living of
discipleship according to the evangelical counsels.
Two Gospel accounts help us to understand this.
In Matthew 8:18–22, Jesus teaches us that to follow
him in the kingdom that he is inaugurating calls for
a commitment that is total and demanding. A scribe
comes to him and says that he will follow Jesus wher-
ever he goes. The reply of Jesus is that he does not
promise his followers economic security but asks of
them total commitment. They are to follow him in
the daily uncertainties of service of the kingdom and

to rely on Divine Providence: "Foxes have holes, and birds of the air have nests; but the Son of man has nowhere to lay his head". Another person (vv. 21–22) tells Jesus that he will follow him after discharging his family obligation to bury his parents. Jesus replies: "Follow me, and leave the dead to bury their own dead." This at first appears shocking, but it is really no more than what was required of a person who had the nazirite vow in the Old Testament (cf. Num 6:6–7) or of a chief priest under the Mosaic law (cf. Lev 21:11). What Jesus is saying is that the urgency of the kingdom takes precedence over family obligations (cf. Mt 10:35–39; 12:46–50; 19:29). That is the sense in which Jesus later says: "Whoever does the will of my Father in heaven is my brother, and sister, and mother" (Mt 12:50). "And every one who has left houses or brothers or sisters or father or mother or children or lands, for my name's sake, will receive a hundredfold, and inherit eternal life" (Mt 19:29).

In a second Gospel account, a rich young man comes to Jesus and asks what good deed he must do to have eternal life. Jesus replies that to enter life, he should keep the commandments. He says to Jesus: "Which?" Our Lord replies: "You shall not kill, You shall not commit adultery, You shall not steal, You shall not bear false witness, Honor your father and mother, and, You shall love your neighbor as yourself." When the young man replies: "All these I have observed; what do I still lack?" Jesus says to him: "If you would be perfect, go, sell what you possess and give to the poor, and you will have treasure in heaven; and come, follow me." We are told that when the young man hears this he goes away sorrowful; for he has great possessions (cf. Mt 19:16–22). We see from this Gospel narrative that Jesus is inviting the young man to prove his love of God and neighbor by selling all he has and distributing it to the poor. Both this life and eternal life are gifts of God, who alone is good. People do not earn salvation by their own performance. It is God's gift. The rich young man does not accept the invitation.

We can see in these two Gospel accounts a distant call to that life which would later in the history of the Church blossom into the consecrated state in which a person lives chastity, poverty, and obedience as a vowed state. We can also see such an invitation to perfect love of him when Jesus later says to his followers: "He who loves father or mother more than me is not worthy of me; and he who loves son or daughter more than me is not worthy of me; and he who does not take his cross and follow me is not worthy of me. He who finds his life will lose it, and he who loses his life for my sake will find it" (Mt 10:37–39). And let us note that our Savior said this to all his followers. People in the consecrated state are striving to follow Christ with radical fidelity.

The earliest Christian community began already

to anticipate what we now associate with the consecrated state. The early Christians had one heart and one soul, and they had a common possession of goods. Those who possessed lands or houses sold them and brought the proceeds, laying them at the feet of the Apostles, and distribution was made to each person according to need. Barnabas was expressly mentioned as one of those who did this, while Ananias and his wife Sapphira indeed sold their piece of property but retained some of the money and made a false declaration before the Apostles. Both of them were struck dead (cf. Acts 4:32—5:1–11). This early practice of detachment from earthly goods and willingness to share in a common life show that some of the elements that were later regarded as expressly characteristic of the consecrated life were already beginning to be lived by the early Christians.

Quite a number of the early Fathers or ecclesiastical writers extol virginity or celibacy vowed for the sake of the kingdom of heaven. Here are examples: In the *Constitutions of the Holy Apostles* we read: "Concerning virginity we have received no commandment; but we leave it to the power of those that are willing" (*Constitutions of the Holy Apostles*, bk. 4, sec. 2; ANF 7:436). Saint Ignatius of Antioch (died ca. 110) writes: "Ye virgins, [be subject] to Christ in purity, not counting marriage an abomination, but desiring that which is better, not for the reproach of wedlock, but for the sake of meditating on the law" (*Epistle to the Philadelphians*, Syriac version, chap. 4; ANF 1:81). Athenagoras, a Greek Christian philosopher and apologist who lived in the second century, testifies: "You would find many among us, both men and women, growing old unmarried, in hope of living in closer communion with God" (*A Plea for the Christians*, chap. 33; ANF 2:146).

Origen (ca. 185–ca. 254), in his *Commentary on Matthew*, writes: "If they 'to whom it is given' can receive this saying about absolute purity, let him who wills ask, obeying and believing Him who said, 'Ask and it shall be given you,' and not doubting about the saying, 'Every one that asketh receiveth' . . . God therefore will give the good gift, perfect purity in celibacy and chastity, to those who ask Him with the whole soul, and with faith, and in prayers without ceasing" (ANF 9:512). Saint Jerome (ca. 347–419/420) is clear: "The Master of the Christian race offers the reward, invites candidates to the course, holds in His hand the prize of virginity, points to the fountain of purity, and cries aloud 'If any man thirst, let him come unto me and drink.' 'He that is able to receive it, let him receive it'" (*Against Jovinianus*, NPNF 2nd series, 6:355). He goes farther: "Let no one think that by this saying ['not all men can receive it', etc.] either fate or fortune is introduced, for those are virgins to whom it is given by God, or that chance has led to this, but it is given to those who have asked for it, who have desired it, who have worked that they might receive it. For it will be given to the one who asks, the seeker will find, and to the one who knocks it will be opened. . . . It is in our power, whether we want to be perfect. But whoever wants to be perfect should sell all that he has . . . and when he has sold, give everything to the poor" (*Commentarium in Evangelium Matthaei*, PL 26:146, 148).

Saint John Chrysostom (ca. 347–407), speaking of the call by Christ to celibacy for the sake of the kingdom of heaven, writes: "And if it is of free choice, one may say, how does He say, at the beginning, 'All men do not receive it, but they to whom it is given?' That you might learn that the conflict is great, not that you should suspect any compulsory allotments. For it is given to those who will it. But He spoke thus to show that much influence from above is needed by him who enters these lists, of which influence he who is willing shall surely partake" (*Homily 62 on Matthew*, PG 58:600; NPNF 1st series 10:384, amended).

Saint Augustine (354–430) speaks of various states of life and extols vowed virginity above the rest: "There are also vows proper for individuals: one voweth to God conjugal chastity, that he will know no other woman besides his wife; so also the woman, that she will know no other man besides her husband. Other men also vow, even though they have used such a marriage, that beyond this they will have no such thing, that they will neither desire nor admit the like: and these men have vowed a greater vow than the former. Others vow even virginity from the beginning of life, that they will even know no such thing as those who having experienced have relinquished: and these men have vowed the greatest vow. Others vow that their house shall be a place of entertainment for all the Saints that may come: a great vow they vow. Another voweth to relinquish all his goods to be distributed to the poor, and go into a community, into a society of the Saints: a great vow he doth vow. 'Vow ye, and pay to the Lord our God.' Let each one vow what he shall have willed to vow; let him give heed to this, that he pay what he hath vowed. If any man doth look back with regard to what he hath vowed to God, it is an evil" (*Exposition on Psalm 76*; NPNF 1st series 8:358–59).

May these sample quotations suffice to show that life according to the three evangelical counsels of chastity, poverty, and obedience is commended by the Apostles, by the Fathers of the Church, and by other teachers and shepherds along the corridors of Church history. From the earliest beginnings of the

Church, the Holy Spirit has given to the Church the grace, not only of the heroic witness of the martyrs, but also of the radical discipleship of virgins, hermits, and anchorites. These disciples were marked by a constant seeking of God, an undivided love for Christ alone, and absolute dedication to the growth of Christ's kingdom.

Saint Anthony of Egypt (251–355) was the first who went to live a secluded life in the desert. Disciples began to join him. A little later, others who were seeking perfection came together with Saint Pachomius (ca. 290–346) as leader. He is considered the founder of Christian cenobitic (or communal) monasticism, and his rule, or book of observances, for monks is the earliest extant. He structured administration of a monastery as a community around the abbot and is said to have founded eleven monasteries numbering more than seven thousand monks and nuns (cf. Encyclopedia Britannica [1985], 9:44–45). Saints Basil of Caesarea, Augustine, Bernard, and Benedict are among the great founders of monastic traditions. In the Middle Ages there arose forms of the consecrated life lived, not in monastic enclosures, but in the midst of the people in the world. Some of these consecrated people engaged in teaching or medical care of the people or in other social services. Church authority followed and guided these developments in radical discipleship of Christ to make sure that those who followed these ways were on the road to holiness of life.

The Second Vatican Council had no hesitation in declaring that "all the faithful of Christ, of whatever rank or status, are called to the fullness of the Christian life and to the perfection of charity" (*Lumen Gentium*, 40). In article 41 of this Dogmatic Constitution on the Church, the Council goes into detail on how different people in the Church live this call to holiness: bishops, priests, other clerics, married people, laborers, the poor, and the sick. Martyrs show a very special degree of holiness because they give their lives for love of God. The Council then goes on to say that "the holiness of the Church is fostered in a special way by the observance of the counsels proposed in the Gospel by Our Lord to His disciples" (*Lumen Gentium*, 42). The Council is speaking of people in the consecrated state who take the vows of chastity, poverty, and obedience in order to follow Christ more closely. It is on this way of life that this book focuses.

Although the consecrated life was not directly established by Christ himself, it developed from his life and teaching. "The counsels", says the Second Vatican Council, "are a divine gift which the Church received from its Lord and which it safeguards with the help of His grace" (*Lumen Gentium*, 43) "Thus, the state which is constituted by the profession of the evangelical counsels, though it is not [part of] the hierarchical structure of the Church, nevertheless, undeniably belongs to its life and holiness" (*Lumen Gentium*, 44). The consecrated state is a way of following Christ's invitation to his disciples to be holy. This explains why the Second Vatican Council in its Dogmatic Constitution on the Church, *Lumen Gentium*, discusses the hierarchical structure of the Church in chapter 3, the lay faithful in chapter 4, the call of the whole Church to holiness in chapter 5, and then only in chapter 6 the consecrated state.

II

Nature and Forms of
the Consecrated State

In the strict sense, every baptized person is by that fact consecrated to God. In the Church, however, the term consecrated state is technically applied to that state of life which people enter by the profession of the three evangelical counsels, or vows of chastity, poverty, and obedience, in a group or community publicly approved by Church authority, as a way of following Christ more closely. "Having dedicated themselves to His honor, the upbuilding of the Church and the salvation of the world by a new and special title, they [those in consecrated life] strive for the perfection of charity in service to the Kingdom of God and, having become an outstanding sign in the Church, they may foretell the heavenly glory" (*Code of Canon Law*, can. 573, §1).

It is not a surprise that the consecrated life in the history of the Church has taken many forms. Common among them all is the profession of the three vows already mentioned. If the consecrated people live in monasteries, they are called monks or nuns.

If they are members of religious orders or congregations in what is technically called "the active life", they are called brothers or sisters. It is normal for monks, nuns, brothers, and sisters to have a distinctive religious habit or dress, although some of them in the last few decades do not insist on this in some parts of the world. Among all these forms of the consecrated life, community living is the norm, and this great value will be considered later in this book.

The Church also recognizes hermits or anchorites as consecrated to God. They take the three vows; they are withdrawn from the world; and they devote their lives to the praise of God and the salvation of the world through the silence of solitude and through constant prayer and penance (cf. CIC can. 603, §1).

The order of virgins is also recognized as a form of the consecrated life. Through their pledge to follow Christ more closely, virgins are consecrated to God, mystically espoused to Christ, and dedicated to the service of the Church. The diocesan bishop consecrates them according to the approved rite. Virgins can be associated together to fulfill their pledge more faithfully and to assist each other in serving the Church in a way that befits their state (cf. CIC can. 604).

Secular institutes are another form of the consecrated life. In these institutes, Christ's faithful who live in the world take the three vows and strive for the perfection of charity and to contribute to the sanctification of the world especially from within. Secular institutes can have as members not only lay faithful but also clerics. "Lay members share in the Church's evangelizing task in the world and of the world through their witness of a Christian life and fidelity toward their consecration, and through their efforts to order temporal things according to God and inform the world by the power of the gospel. Also, they cooperate in serving the ecclesial community, according to their particular secular way of life. Clerical members through the witness of their consecrated life, especially in the presbyteriate, help their brothers by their special apostolic charity and in their sacred ministry among the people of God they bring about the sanctification of the world" (CIC can. 713). Together with Saint John Paul II, the Church thanks the Holy Spirit for this charism of the new expression of the consecrated life in the form of the secular institutes. In particular, their lay members, through their own specific blending of presence in the world and consecration, "*seek to make present in society the newness and power of Christ's Kingdom*, striving to transfigure the world from within by the power of the Beatitudes" (*Vita Consecrata*, 10).

There are also in the Church societies of apostolic life. They are of many types. They pursue specific apostolic or missionary ends. Some of them make an explicit commitment to the evangelical counsels. But they are not religious institutes, nor are they secular institutes (cf. *Vita Consecrata*, 11). These societies are not under consideration in this book.

"From the very beginning of the Church", says the Second Vatican Council, "men and women have set about following Christ with greater freedom and imitating Him more closely through the practice of the evangelical counsels" (*Perfectae Caritatis*, 1). This radical way of living the Gospel on this earth is a "particularly profound and fruitful way of sharing in *Christ's mission*, in imitation of the example of Mary of Nazareth" (*Vita Consecrata*, 18). It is also a powerful message to all other members of the Church and to society as a whole, because a consecrated person sacrifices the three best things on earth, marriage, possessions, and doing one's own will, for the sake of the kingdom of heaven. As the Second Vatican Council puts it, "the profession of the evangelical counsels, then, appears as a sign which can and ought to attract all the members of the Church to an effective and prompt fulfillment of the duties of their Christian vocation. . . . The religious state clearly manifests that the Kingdom of God and its needs, in a very special way, are raised above all earthly considerations" (*Lumen Gentium*, 44).

When Pope Francis met with the members of the

executive council of the Union of Superiors General of religious men on November 29, 2013, he observed that a radical life is required of all Christians but that religious are called to follow the Lord in a special way. "They are the men and women who awaken the world. Consecrated life is prophecy. God asks us to leave the nest that restrains and to be sent to the edges of the world, avoiding the temptations to domesticate them. This is the most effective way to imitate the Lord" (in *L'Osservatore romano*, weekly English ed., December 6, 2013, p. 7).

It is to be noted that the work that a consecrated religious person carries out, like teaching or nursing or doing other social work, is secondary to who the consecrated man or woman is. A teacher, a catechist, a nurse, or other social worker could carry out some of those practical works. But for a religious, the life of consecration has priority and is the apostolic and spiritual basis and fount of those external works. As the *Code of Canon Law* puts it, in institutes dedicated to apostolic works, "Apostolic action is always to proceed from an intimate union with God, and it is to confirm and foster that union" (CIC can. 675, §2). The consecrated life is about union with God, service of God, knowledge of God, having God as the absolute in one's life, and living for God. The consecrated person gives God everything. In that life of total consecration, service of neighbor has its proper place. External works become a manifestation of that love of God and neighbor. As we proceed in this reflection, it will become clearer and clearer that, as Saint John Paul II puts it, "the profession of the evangelical counsels is *an integral part of the Church's life* and a much-needed incentive toward ever greater fidelity to the Gospel" (*Vita Consecrata*, 3).

III

The Consecrated Life
in Numbers

Numbers tend to be dry. They do not say everything or even what is most primary in the life of the Church, which is holiness. The life of the Church is God's work. It is in itself not measurable in numbers, statistics, or human means of reckoning and census taking. Nevertheless, because the life of the Church is also incarnate in space and time, it has human aspects such as numbers.

A numerical reckoning of Church personnel, such as lay faithful, clerics, religious, or institutions, has its usefulness, provided it is not regarded as an indication of the power of the Church or of her strength or vitality. It is holiness of life that is the measure of the Church's performance. Holiness cannot be measured in human terms, although we can perceive something of the witness given by holy people.

It is also useful to remark that when we speak of Church personnel, one should not think only of clerics and consecrated people. There are also members of societies of apostolic life, permanent deacons, catechists, lay missionaries, and others. And we must not forget the ecclesial movements and associations that the Holy Spirit raises to answer various needs of the mission of the Church. This book is focusing on the consecrated people.

It is also to be noted that the religious state is not a third state between the clerics and the lay faithful. Rather, religious are clerics or lay people who are consecrated in an institute with the three evangelical counsels as its base. A religious institute is clerical if "by reason of the purpose or design intended by its founder or in virtue of legitimate tradition, it is under the supervision of clerics, it assumes the exercise of sacred orders, and it is recognized as such by church authority. . . . An institute is called lay if recognized as such by church authority, by virtue of its nature, character and purpose, it has a proper function defined by the founder or by legitimate tradition which does not include the exercise of sacred orders" (CIC can. 588). In simple language, this means that all religious men are brothers, but some religious men are also priests. This will be reflected in the statistics we are about to supply.

The following figures from the *Statistics Yearbook of the Church 2011* (p. 77) give an idea of how many consecrated people we have in the Church, in comparison with other Church personnel, as of December 31, 2011:

World population	6,933,310,000
Catholics	1,213,591,000
Bishops	5,132
Diocesan Priests	281,346
Religious Priests	132,072
All Priests	413,418
Permanent Deacons	40,914
Religious Men (Brothers)	55,085
Religious Women	713,206
Secular Institute Members	25,277
Lay Missionaries	381,722
Catechists	3,125,235

It is also interesting to know which seven religious orders or congregations had the highest number of members in December 2011:

Jesuits	17,287
Salesians	5,573
Franciscans Minor	14,123
Franciscans Capuchins	10,786
Franciscans Conventuals	4,289
Redemptorists	5,338
Dominicans	4,459

(cf. G. P. Salvini, in *La Civiltà Cattolica*, October 5, 2013, p. 70).

Of interest also is the distribution of professed women by continents at the same date, December 31, 2011:

Africa	67,863
North and South America	190,683
Asia	167,423
Europe	278,583
Oceania	8,654
World Total:	713,206

(cf. *Statistical Yearbook of the Church 2011*, p. 224).

We can also remark that in 1978 there were 75,802 religious brothers who were not priests, but their number went down to 55,085 in 2011; while the number of religious women went from 990,000 in 1978 to 713,206 in 2011. In both cases, the numbers went down in Europe, the Americas, and Oceania and went up in Africa and Asia. The traditional forms of religious life have known the crisis of decrease in numbers, even though the diminution speed is now less pronounced. This decrease in number is most noticeable in women's religious congregations, although not so much in monasteries. This has involved the closing of some religious houses, convents, and schools, with the allied problem or challenge of carrying on the works earlier done by the sisters. Some of the reasons for this decrease in number are growing secularization, greater preoccupation with material things, and fewer children in families. We cannot go into all these reasons here.

This is also a suitable place to express the deep gratitude of the peoples of Asia, Latin America, and Africa, who in the past five hundred years have been evangelized by members of religious orders or congregations, at great sacrifice. Most missionaries have been religious or members of societies of apostolic life. In many countries in Africa in the past two hundred years, the Missionary Fathers of the Holy Spirit, the Society of African Missions, the Jesuits, the Missionaries of Africa, and the Comboniani Fathers have been particularly active. Among the women religious, the Missionary Sisters of the Holy Rosary, the Our Lady of Apostles Sisters, the Loreto Sisters, and the Holy Child Sisters have done very well and have helped to give life to sisters' congregations founded in the new mission countries.

It is also important to record that many religious congregations have arisen in territories evangelized only in the past two hundred years. In my own country, Nigeria, one can think, for example, of the Handmaids of the Holy Child Jesus, of the Sisters of the Immaculate Heart of Mary Mother of Christ, of the Sisters of the Eucharistic Heart of Jesus, the Fatima Sisters, the Daughters of Divine Love, and the Daughters of Mary Mother of Mercy. These religious families receive many candidates. Benedictine, Cistercian, and Carmelite monasteries are also happily growing. The monasteries of monks are also making good progress. Among the religious brothers can be mentioned the Sons of Mary Mother of Mercy and the Brothers of Saint Stephen. Two prominent societies of priests in Africa founded for missionary work deserve to be mentioned. They are the Apostles of Jesus, with their generalate in Nairobi, and the Missionary Society of Saint Paul, centered in Abuja. The reader will notice that I have mentioned only a small number of religious orders or congregations and a couple of societies, leaving out others that could very well have been included. I have listed those few simply to show how God's grace has borne much fruit in areas of recent evangelization.

The Holy Spirit guides the Church. He has raised up new forms of response to the Gospel call in the past fifty years since the Second Vatican Council. Examples are the Catholic movements, associations, and societies of apostolic life. These have generally manifested surprising vitality. Some of them have branches that are forms of the consecrated life or that approximate them. We do not know what surprises the Spirit of God may have in reserve for the future.

IV

Church Appreciation for the Consecrated State

Our Holy Mother the Church in many ways shows her love of the consecrated life and her appreciation of it. It is Church authority that, under the inspiration of the Holy Spirit, interprets the three evangelical counsels, regulates their practice, and establishes stable norms for living according to them. The same Church authority examines and approves the constitutions and rules proposed by the various founders, together with any eventual modifications, and thus guarantees to the members a proven way to follow Christ more closely. It supervises and protects the religious families "so that they may grow and flourish according to the spirit of their founders" (*Lumen Gentium*, 45; cf. also CIC can. 576).

A major area of Church responsibility is the examination and approval of new expressions of the consecrated life, to see how authentic they are and, if they are mere repetitions of existing forms, to "prevent the proliferation of institutions similar to one another, with the consequent risk of a harmful fragmentation into excessively small groups" (*Vita Consecrata*, 12). *The Code of Canon Law* is very attentive to various aspects of the religious life, such as establishment and suppression, governance, temporal goods, admission and formation of candidates, obligations and rights, apostolate, separation of members and conferences of major superiors. One hundred thirty-seven canons (CIC cann. 573–709) are dedicated to religious institutes, while twenty-one canons (cann. 710–30) pertain to secular institutes. The role of the diocesan bishop in encouraging these institutes and guaranteeing their good functioning is recalled many times by Church law (see, for example, canons 567, 586, 591, 594, 595, 603, 604, 605, 609, 611, 612, 616, 630, 637, 644, 678, 679, 681, and 783). "Thus, Bishops are asked to welcome and esteem the charisms of the consecrated life, and to give them a place in the pastoral plans of the Diocese" (*Vita Consecrata*, 48).

It is impressive how much attention the Church has given to the consecrated life since the Second Vatican Council, in major documents from the Council, from the pope, and from three of the Congregations at his service. Here is a brief list:

Vatican II: *Lumen Gentium*, chapter six, in 1964

Vatican II: *Perfectae Caritatis*, in 1965

Paul VI: *Evangelica Testificatio*, the Apostolic Exhortation on the Renewal of the Religious Life according to the Teaching of the Second Vatican Council, in 1971

John Paul II: Post-Synodal Apostolic Exhortation *Vita Consecrata*, in 1996

John Paul II: *Message for the I World Day for Consecrated Life*, in 1997.

The Congregation for Bishops and the Congregation for Religious issued jointly: *Mutuae Relationes*, on relations between bishops and religious, in 1978.

The Congregation for Institutes of Consecrated Life and Societies of Apostolic Life has issued the following documents:

The Contemplative Dimension of Religious Life, in 1980

Fraternal Life in Community, in 1994

Inter-Institute Collaboration for Formation, in 1999

Starting Afresh from Christ, in 2002

The Service of Authority and Obedience, in 2008.

The Congregation for Catholic Education issued two documents that concern the consecrated people directly:

Consecrated Persons and Their Mission in Schools, in 2002

Educating Together in Catholic Schools: A Shared Mission between Consecrated Persons and the Lay Faithful, in 2007.

Moreover, there was an Ordinary Assembly of the Synod of Bishops in 1994 on *The Consecrated Life and*

Its Role in the Church and in the World. The discussion of any theme by the world Assembly of the Synod of Bishops always gives a heightened visibility to that dimension in the life of the Church.

The inescapable conclusion from all these initiatives is that the Church gives considerable attention to the consecrated life.

The special link between consecrated people and the Church needs to be appreciated. The Second Vatican Council is very explicit: "The Church not only raises the religious profession to the dignity of a canonical state by her approval, but even manifests that this profession is a state consecrated to God by the liturgical setting of that profession. The Church itself, by the authority given to it by God, accepts the vows of the newly professed. It begs aid and grace from God for them by its public prayer. It commends them to God, imparts a spiritual blessing on them and accompanies their self-offering by the Eucharistic sacrifice" (*Lumen Gentium*, 45). Although what has just been quoted was said expressly of the religious state, it applies equally to other forms of the consecrated state, such as hermits, the order of virgins, and secular institutes. A priest can indeed preside over the rite of profession with the Mass that goes with it. But it is clear that the ecclesial nature of the event becomes more manifest when it is the bishop, the head of the particular Church or diocese, who presides.

The Second Vatican Council, as a consequence of the ecclesial nature of the consecrated state, says that "All institutes should share in the life of the Church, adapting as their own and implementing in accordance with their own characteristics the Church's undertakings and aims in matters biblical, liturgical, dogmatic, pastoral, ecumenical, missionary and social" (*Perfectae Caritatis*, 2). "Since the Church has accepted their surrender of self they should realize they are also dedicated to its service" (ibid., 5). Since as consecrated persons they have been joined to the Church and her mystery in a special way, members of the consecrated state should work to implement and strengthen the kingdom of Christ in souls and to extend that kingdom according to their various charisms and approved constitutions and rules.

In his encyclical letter *Mysterium Fidei*, on the Holy Eucharist, issued just before the last session of the Second Vatican Council in 1965, Pope Paul VI shows special appreciation of the role of religious as adorers of Jesus in the Holy Eucharist: "This zeal at prayer and at devoting oneself to God for the sake of the unity of the Church is something that religious, both men and women, should regard as very specially their own since they are bound in a special way to adoration of the Blessed Sacrament, and they have, by virtue of the vows they have pronounced, become a kind of crown set around it here on earth" (*Mysterium Fidei*, 71).

On June 29, 1971, the same pope published *Evangelica Testificatio*, the Apostolic Exhortation on the Renewal of the Religious Life according to the Teaching of the Second Vatican Council. His esteem for the religious life and its contribution to the life of the Church is unambiguously stated in paragraph 4: "Could you but understand all the esteem and the affection that We have for you in the name of Christ Jesus! We commend you to Our most dear brothers in the episcopate who, together with their collaborators in the priesthood, realize their own responsibility in regard to the religious life. And we ask all the laity to whom 'secular duties and activities belong properly, although not exclusively' to understand what a strong help you are for them in the striving for that holiness, to which they also are called by their baptism in Christ, to the glory of the Father."

Religious and other consecrated persons have an important role in the evangelizing mission of the Church. Pope Paul VI could not have forgotten this role in his apostolic exhortation *Evangelii Nuntiandi*, which he issued after the 1974 Synod on Evangelization in the Modern World. Among the workers for evangelization, he says of religious: "Religious, for their part, find in their consecrated life a privileged means of effective evangelization. At the deepest level of their being they are caught up in the dynamism of the Church's life, which is thirsty for the divine Absolute and called to holiness. It is to this holiness that they bear witness. They embody the Church in her desire to give herself completely to the radical demands of the beatitudes. By their lives they are a sign of total availability to God, the Church and the brethren" (*Evangelii Nuntiandi*, 69).

Pope Benedict XVI in many documents and addresses manifests great esteem for the consecrated life. Let us select four examples. In his Post-Synodal Apostolic Exhortation *Verbum Domini*, after the Synod on the Word of God in the Life and Mission of the Church, he rejoices that the great monastic tradition has always considered meditation on Sacred Scripture to be an essential part of that specific spirituality, particularly in the form of *lectio divina*. "The world today", he says, "is often excessively caught up in outward activities and risks losing its bearings. Contemplative men and women, by their lives of prayer, attentive hearing and meditation on God's Word, remind us that man does not live by bread alone but by every word that comes from the mouth of God" (*Verbum Domini*, 83). After the Synod on the Holy Eucharist, in his Post-Synodal Apostolic Exhortation *Sacramentum Caritatis*, he extols "the prophetic witness of consecrated men and women, who find in the celebration of the Eucharist and in eucharistic adoration the strength necessary for the radical following of Christ, obedient, poor and chaste" (*Sacramentum Caritatis*, 81).

The Second Assembly of the Synod of Bishops for Africa in 2008 had as its theme Reconciliation, Justice and Peace in Africa and the Role of the Church. In the apostolic exhortation that followed that synod, Pope Benedict singles out the contribution of consecrated people in their witness to these virtues. "Through the vows of chastity, poverty and obedience", he says, "the life of consecrated persons becomes a prophetic witness. Hence they can be examples in the area of reconciliation, justice and peace, even in circumstances marked by great tension. Community life shows us that it is possible to live as brothers and sisters, and to be united even when coming from different ethnic or racial backgrounds" (*Africae Munus*, 117). Pope Benedict praises religious for their great charity when shown concretely, especially to the poor. In his very first encyclical letter, he extols "the immense initiatives of human welfare and Christian formation, aimed above all at the very poor, who became the object of care firstly for the monastic and mendicant orders, and later for the various male and female religious institutes all through the history of the Church. The figures of saints such as Francis of Assisi, Ignatius of Loyola, John of God, Camillus of Lellis, Vincent de Paul, Louise de Marillac, Giuseppe B. Cottolengo, John Bosco, Luigi

Orione, Teresa of Calcutta—to name but a few—
stand out as lasting models of social charity for all
people of good will. The saints are the true bearers
of light within history, for they are men and women
of faith, hope and love" (*Deus Caritas Est*, 40).

For an institute of the consecrated life to answer all
such calls, it has to remain faithful to the spirit of
its founder. The Church is also sensitive to the fact
that each institute should have canonical autonomy
within the family of the Church. "Each Institute",
says Saint John Paul II, "is recognized as having *a
rightful autonomy*, enabling it to follow its own discipline and to keep intact its spiritual and apostolic
patrimony. It is the responsibility of local Ordinar-
ies to preserve and safeguard this autonomy" (*Vita
Consecrata*, 48; cf. also CIC can. 586). It is obvious
that constant dialogue between bishops and major religious and other superiors is most valuable in promoting mutual understanding, which is a necessary
precondition for effective cooperation, especially in
matters pastoral in nature (cf. *Vita Consecrata*, 50).
Pope Francis, speaking to the Union of Major Superiors, says that he knows from experience the possible dilemmas, but he adds that "we bishops must
understand that consecrated people are not materi-
als for help, but they are gifts that enrich the dioceses" (in *L'Osservatore romano*, weekly English ed., December 6, 2013, p. 7). He asks the Congregation for

Institutes of Consecrated Life and Societies of Apostolic Life to revise and bring up to date the 1978 document *Mutuae Relationes*, which gives directives on relations between bishops and religious in the diocese. He says that if the charisms of the religious institutes are well understood, the institutes will be properly inserted into the dioceses and will not be regarded simply as useful instruments.

Saint John Paul II considers the value of the consecrated life to be special. He states that the roles of the lay faithful and those of bishops and priests are of course indispensable. But he then adds significantly that, "as a way of showing forth the Church's holiness, *it is to be recognized that the consecrated life* [italics in the original], which mirrors Christ's own way of life, *has an objective superiority*. Precisely for this reason, it is an especially rich manifestation of Gospel values and a more complete expression of the Church's purpose, which is the sanctification of humanity. The consecrated life proclaims and in a certain way anticipates the future age, when the fullness of the Kingdom of heaven, already present in its first fruits and in mystery, will be achieved" (*Vita Consecrata*, 32).

The people of God show their appreciation for the consecrated life in many ways. They come to religious profession ceremonies, sometimes over long distances. They surround with prayer their relatives or friends who are pronouncing their vows. They bring gifts. Photographs are taken to immortalize the occasion. Those who cannot be physically present send supportive letters, telephone calls, and emails. Sometimes the parish council, under the leadership of the parish priest, arranges a Mass of thanksgiving and a solemn reception for the professed or the jubilarian. In one religious congregation, the other sisters write their messages of congratulations to the member celebrating her silver or golden jubilee, and these messages are bound together and handed over to the jubilarian. Bishops make every effort to preside over profession ceremonies. The diocesan newspaper gives an inspiring report with fitting photographs.

The people at various levels, like family, village, or parish, sometimes put in writing their good wishes, expectations, and prayers. Here is what the family members wrote of one sister who was celebrating her first profession silver jubilee: "The challenge was as daunting as any difficulty could possibly be, but Sister had the heart of a lioness and the will power of an elephant, with the defiant can-do attitude in which nothing appeared impossible to her. Her determination was as strong as steel, and her zealous courage legendary."

In the ceremony of the final vows of a sister, her biological sisters cried when she was pronouncing her vows and said to her after the Mass: "Congratulations. You are now a mother in the Church. Pray for us. Be a good religious and do not disgrace our family."

To another sister who was also celebrating her silver jubilee, the people wrote: "What a memorable day! We celebrate with joy the twenty-five years of your espousal with Christ. Your religious vocation has been inspirational, and your meritorious services to God and humanity exemplary. Your saintly composure and smiles radiate God's love to people around you. We thank God for giving you the abundant blessings, courage, energy, wisdom, knowledge, and inspiration that helped you to accomplish these faithful spirit-filled years in his vineyard."

Another extended family encouraged their sister jubilarian in rather clear terms: "The fact that you are celebrating your silver jubilee of religious profession does not mean that you have reached the end of the journey. In fact, you have just begun, and so do not relax; there is need for you now to rekindle your zeal. You should never allow your health condition to discourage you. One thing you should realize is that sick people are very close to the Lord. So instead of being unhappy with your condition, see yourself as privileged and continue to love the Lord with all your being." We must admit that this is not a bad sermon for relatives to preach!

V

The Three
Evangelical Counsels

The reason for taking the three vows of chastity, poverty, and obedience is to follow Christ more closely. Saint John the Evangelist already warned us not to give our love to the world and what it has to offer: "Do not love the world or the things in the world. If any one loves the world, love for the Father is not in him. For all that is in the world, the lust of the flesh and the lust of the eyes and the pride of life, is not of the Father but is of the world. And the world passes away, and the lust of it; but he who does the will of God abides for ever" (1 Jn 2:15–17). Pleasure, possessions, and power are not bad in themselves. They can enhance human life. But when they are chased without moderation, they lead to evil. Indeed, every evil people are capable of committing can be traced to one of these "lusts". The three evangelical counsels seek to root out these lusts so that the human soul is freer in seeking God. The three vows are free sacrifices of the three best things on earth—marriage, possessions, and doing one's own will—in order to follow Jesus in a more radical way, according to the example of his own life on earth. Let us now reflect on each of these counsels.

Chastity as a virtue is acceptance of God's will concerning the origins of human life, respect for marriage and the family, and therefore the right use of the sexual faculty only within lawful marriage. This virtue is binding on all human beings. Chastity is about true love for other people: "Thou shalt love", which also contains a negative element, "Thou shalt not use". This virtue is about loving kindness toward other people. It rejects any type of "utilization" of that person. Chastity affirms the value of the other person. It is a profound Yes to the love of God. The love of God touches us and provokes a response of love. Saint John Paul II says that "Love is . . . the fundamental and innate vocation of every human being" (*Familiaris Consortio*, 11). And the Pontifical Council for the Family makes the important observation that "Chastity is . . . that spiritual energy capable of defending love from the perils of selfishness and aggressiveness and able to advance it towards its full realization" (*The Truth and Meaning of Human Sexuality*, 4 [December 8, 1995]).

As a vow, chastity is love of God right up to the sacrifice of marriage and all that it entails for the sake of the kingdom of heaven (cf. Mt 19:12). It liberates the human heart in a unique way and causes it to burn with greater love for God and mankind, as Saint Paul explains to the Corinthians (cf. 1 Cor 7:32–35). For the person who takes the vow of chastity, the aim is to liberate, not to restrict the power to love. For the consecrated person, this vowed state is an image of the mystical union between Christ and his Bride, the Church. "The *joyful living of perfect chastity* [is] a witness to the power of God's love manifested in the weakness of the human condition" (*Vita Consecrata*, 88). "Chastity is decisively positive", says Pope Paul VI. "It witnesses to preferential love for the Lord and symbolizes in the most eminent and absolute way the mystery of the union of the Mystical Body with its Head, the union of the Bride with her eternal Bridegroom. Finally, it reaches, transforms and imbues with a mysterious likeness to Christ man's being in its most hidden depths" (*Evangelica Testificatio*, 13).

For all this to be realized in the life of the consecrated person, it is necessary that the person be equipped with the needed discipline together with emotional and psychological maturity. He should not ignore those mortifications and ascetical helps which history, common sense, and the examples of the saints have proved useful or even necessary. The Second Vatican Council also draws attention to the fact "that chastity is guarded more securely when true brotherly love flourishes in the common life of the community" (*Perfectae Caritatis*, 12).

One dimension of the living of vowed chastity that needs to be specially mentioned is spiritual fatherhood or motherhood. Although this concept can be wrongly interpreted and it can be exaggerated, there is an important truth in it. The consecrated celibate is not barren. He is not an ecclesiastical bachelor or spinster. By their committed love for other people, consecrated people encourage and nourish the divine life in those people and help them to grow in that life. They become in a way spiritual fathers and mothers. Why was Blessed Teresa of Calcutta so well known and loved? She had intense love of God, and this overflowed into love of neighbor. The Scriptures tell us that perfection consists in love of God and of our neighbor. To be more exact, perfection is love of God that extends to the neighbor. The motive is in God. My neighbor is my way to God. Jesus tells us that the second commandment is like the first (cf. Mt 22:39). Saint John explains: "If any one says, 'I love God,' and hates his brother, he is a liar; for he who does not love his brother whom he has seen, cannot love God whom he has not seen" (1 Jn 4:20).

Blessed Teresa of Calcutta so loved her neighbor, indeed the poorest of the poor, that many saw her as their spiritual mother. She gave many people the conviction that they were loved, that God loved them. Once Mother Teresa was caring for a sick and poor person. The man asked her who she was. Mother Teresa told him her name. The man replied: "No, you are the smile of God." When Mother Teresa died, the newspapers in India carried the eloquent heading: "Mother is dead." Everyone in India knew who "Mother" was. The consecrated person who is dry and unloving is not living properly the spirit of the vow of chastity. The living of vowed chastity, understood as consecrated total love, is an important element of the love that the consecrated person has for other people.

An unbiased observer sees the great good that the noble living of this vow has brought to Church and society. "The consecrated life must present to today's world examples of chastity lived by men and women who show balance, self-mastery, an enterprising spirit, and psychological and affective maturity" (*Vita Consecrata*, 88). Think of Saints Thomas Aquinas, Francis of Assisi, Clare of Assisi, Teresa of Avila, Ignatius of Loyola, Francis Xavier, John Bosco, and Thérèse of Lisieux, and of Blessed Cyprian Michael Tansi and Mother Teresa of Calcutta. These saints had no doubt many qualities that made them great and enabled them to accomplish much for Church and society. Their singleness of purpose can be considered as connected to their vowed celibate state. The flaming examples of these holy religious are priceless incentives to everyone else to live that chastity which corresponds to that person's state of life. "We are in fact dealing here with a precious gift which the Father imparts to certain people. This gift, fragile and vulnerable because of human weakness, remains open to the contradictions of mere reason and is in part incomprehensible to those to whom the light of the Word Incarnate has not revealed how he who loses his life for Him will find it" (Paul VI, *Evangelica Testificatio*, 15).

The vow of *poverty* is taken by consecrated persons in imitation of Jesus, who lived poor and who advised a would-be follower to sell all he had, distribute to the poor, and then come and follow him. He added: "Foxes have holes, and birds of the air have nests; but the Son of man has nowhere to lay his head" (Mt 8:20). The person who takes this vow entrusts self to Divine Providence and strives to avoid undue worry about the future (cf. Mt 6:25). Each religious institute is expected to give corporate witness to poverty and to show love for the poor and the needy (cf. Mt 19:21; 25:34–46; Jas 2:15–16; 1 Jn 3:17).

By the vow of poverty, people attest that God is the true wealth of the human heart. They challenge the idolatry of money and encourage active involvement in the promotion of solidarity and charity and in the preferential option for the poor. They also help to train young people and future leaders to seek to eliminate the structures of oppression and to help the poor get out of situations of poverty. Aware of the universal destination of earthly goods by God the Creator (cf. *Gaudium et Spes*, 69), they ask themselves what they can do to promote a fairer distribution of international aid and of the goods of the earth.

There are acceptable differences in the way the vow of poverty is lived in the various orders, congregations, and institutes around the world, taking into consideration cultural practices, work demands, and approved customs. For example, a nun in a Trappist monastery does not need to have the pocket money that a medical sister is expected to have. A religious who is a student needs to be able to pay for books, transportation to school, lodging, and similar needs. A member of a secular institute needs funds in accordance with the nature of his vocation. Each family of the consecrated life works out how the vow of poverty is to be practiced by its members. Some general remarks, however, can be made on the practice of poverty.

Many people habitually find their identity secured by their material possessions and social standing. The vow of poverty challenges this and asks for sacrifice. The consecrated person has to learn, even if gradually, to find his identity in personal relationship with Jesus Christ and in spiritual realities that go beyond material possessions. When such a person is fully engaged in some practical apostolate, he should be vigilant, because this desire to seek security through material things may reappear in his new areas of work.

In a way, the virtue of humility can be located and examined under the vow of poverty. After all, the vow of poverty includes the sacrifice of public prominence. In the world, people understandably seek full self-expression and exposure to the public, especially when they are seeking political office. Is the consecrated person content to have his life hidden with Christ in God? (cf. Col 3:3). Jesus tells us that unless we are converted and become as children, we shall not enter the kingdom of heaven (cf. Mt 18:3). He prays: "I thank you, Father, Lord of heaven and earth, that you have hidden these things from the wise and understanding and revealed them to infants" (Mt 11:25). Does the consecrated person see himself among the little ones? It is not so much the lack of material goods that makes such consecrated people happy but, rather, the spirit of seeing oneself as small, as not self-sufficient, as dependent, not on self or personal resources, but on God.

For some consecrated persons, a bigger sacrifice is demanded by having to ask permission to go somewhere or to obtain money they need, or think they need, for a particular matter. Superiors cannot altogether remove this sacrifice, but their manner of looking after the needs of their colleagues can reduce the pinch of this humiliation. It is not proper for a consecrated person to be tempted to go against the rules by not declaring some of the gifts received.

Some religious unnecessarily compare themselves to diocesan priests. They ask why a diocesan priest can keep the gifts he received at his ordination or jubilee, while the religious has to declare all gifts and hand them over to the superior. The answer is to ask such a religious whether the vow of poverty was explained to him during the novitiate. Moreover, every family of the consecrated life can discuss and develop its own customs on how to handle gifts and how much pocket money each member may retain.

The whole area of relationships with parents, brothers and sisters, cousins and other members of the biological family needs careful attention. One can imagine the pain a consecrated person feels when, for example, his mother is very poor and is living in a shack. While the mother did not take the vow of poverty, the son or daughter who is consecrated has no personal money. In some cases, the religious family of the consecrated person has to help. In fact, some religious congregations that run old people's homes see it as their duty to receive very poor parents of their members into such homes. What, however, is not acceptable is for relatives to expect their consecrated son or daughter to bring them Church money or for these relatives to presume they have the right to be maintained with Church funds, including the payment of university fees for young relatives.

The practice of the vow of poverty also poses challenges and questions regarding the possession or use of such items as cell phones, computers, cameras, and television sets. Every family of the consecrated life has to work out its own policy. In many areas of the world today, the use of such machines is regarded as normal or even necessary and is taken for granted. Some religious congregations that have members in several countries cut travel costs by holding conferences or meetings by telephone and the use of the internet (computer). The needs of a member of a congregation of medical sisters are different from those of nuns or monks in a monastery. A question, however, can be raised when the life-style of some consecrated persons is higher in comparison to that of many people in that particular cultural area, so that people begin to ask what these consecrated people have really sacrificed. How the vow of poverty is lived requires occasional review in each area of the world.

Poverty is primarily a mental attitude of detachment from riches, from the superfluous, from the desire to possess, from the desire to be the center and the deciding person of what happens. If a consecrated person maneuvers through a long string of "permissions" finally to arrive at having and using whatever he desires, would such a person not be going against the spirit of this vow? And what of the consecrated person who is often complaining and is rarely satisfied with this food, that article of clothing, this room furniture, or that little sum of money for a journey? Impatience at monotonous assignments and humble tasks can also be signs that a person still has a long way to go to live this vow and virtue. Superiors can also ask themselves whether they give personal example, for instance, by not allowing the community to mount too expensive a celebration in honor of the superior.

Here tribute needs to be paid to many religious who spend their lives for the poor and with the poor. Some religious sisters, living the charism of their religious family, have even sacrificed their lives in their service of patients with diseases like ebola. Many HIV/AIDS patients around the world are looked after by such sisters. When the Gospel is lived without compromise, it casts light on the hearts of individuals. It can also expose the structures that promote injustice and keep the poor in their poverty. The rich and powerful generally lack credibility when they preach to the poor and powerless, even when the words they employ are correct. Could that not be one of the reasons why Pope Francis has unassailable credibility?

Obedience is the vow by which religious and other consecrated persons sacrifice their own wills in order to unite themselves with greater steadiness and security to the saving will of God. In this, they strive to follow Christ, who gave his life as a ransom for many (cf. Mt 20:28; Jn 10:14–18).

Vowed obedience, if properly practiced, does not diminish the dignity of the human person but, rather, leads it to maturity. Dialogue is of great help so that members of a community carry out the duties assigned to them with all their gifts of nature and grace. Dialogue, however, should not be reduced to an endless filibuster aimed at eventually wearing down the superior and getting him to surrender. It should be a sincere and calm but honest examination of the pros and cons of a certain course of action. Saint Benedict instructs the abbot that when an important problem arises, the whole community in the monastery is to be called to a meeting. The abbot sets forth the matter to be examined, listens to everyone, and later reflects on what seems the most useful course to follow. Saint Benedict adds that often the Lord reveals the best solution to the youngest (cf. *Rule of St. Benedict*, chap. 3). No matter how long such dialogue goes on, it never removes the responsibility of the superior in the end to decide on what has to be done (cf. *Perfectae Caritatis*, 14).

It can sometimes happen that a religious or other

consecrated person feels that what the superior has ordered is beyond his strength or that it may do harm to him, to other people, or to the community. In that case, the person has the right, and sometimes even the duty, to bring the matter to the superior. It is then the duty of the superior to give the person a careful listening. If the matter is complex, the superior may wish to consult others. The aim of the superior should be to seek what is God's will for that consecrated person. There comes a time when the superior is satisfied that all sides of the question have been sufficiently examined. The superior finally gives a directive to the person in question. This latter should accept and carry it out and trust in God's protection in ways that God knows best. Obedience, in the final analysis, is built on faith, love, and trust in Divine Providence.

Members in a community of consecrated persons can ask themselves whether they are really ready to sacrifice their will and whether they see orders or directives from their superiors as God speaking to them. If any of them resorts to murmuring or to promoting discontent, how can they expect God's blessing? On the other hand, the superior should also examine his conscience and methods. Does the superior see his position as an opportunity to do what he likes? Does the superior sufficiently appreciate that any manifestation of vindictiveness or lack of love distorts the sense of the voice of God in the superior and that injustice makes it difficult to make the needed sacrifices and to obey orders? Is there a deliberate effort on the part of the superior to look for the will of God and to transmit it to the members in question? Does the style of the superior inspire joy, hope, and courage or, rather, tension, discontent, and dishonesty of character in the community? Does the superior see authority as service rather than domination, considering that our Divine Master washed the feet of his Apostles and taught them to behave likewise? Does the style of the superior encourage the members of the community to say with the Psalmist: "Great peace have those who love your law, nothing can make them stumble" (Ps 119:165)?

"Authority and obedience", says Pope Paul VI, "are exercised in the service of the common good as two complementary aspects of the same participation in Christ's offering. For those in authority, it is a matter of serving in their brothers the design of the Father's love; while, in accepting their directives, the religious follow our Master's example and cooperate in the work of salvation. Thus, far from being in opposition to one another, authority and individual liberty go together in the fulfillment of God's will, which is sought fraternally through a trustful dialogue between the superior and his brother, in the case of a personal situation, or through a general agreement regarding what concerns the whole community" (*Evangelica Testificatio*, 25).

As for those members of the consecrated life who struggle with the effort to sacrifice their will, it is salutary to reflect on how, in the Old Testament, God meted out severe punishment to those who disobeyed or who showed contempt for proper authority. Aaron and Miriam complained against Moses, and Miriam was turned into a leper on the spot (cf. Num 12:1–10). The men who reconnoitered the promised land and advised against going into it were struck dead (cf. Num 14:37). Korah, Dathan, and Abiram rebelled against Moses. They and 250 Levites were consumed by the ground opening and closing in on them (cf. Num 16:1–34). Do we need more evidence that God wants us to respect the authority he has set up?

Of course the consecrated person obeys, not out of fear of God's immediate punishment, but rather from motives of faith, love, and trust. Beautiful and luminous examples of obedience are given us in the Gospel. Mary and Joseph obeyed the decree of Caesar and traveled to Bethlehem for the census just when the Child Jesus was expected (cf. Lk 2:1–4). They obeyed the Mosaic law to have Jesus circumcised (cf. Lk 2:21) and to present him in the temple (cf. Lk 2:22–24). Even the flight into Egypt was an act of obedience, and Joseph did not ask questions (cf. Mt 2:13–23). That Jesus accompanied Mary and Joseph to the Passover celebration when he reached the age of twelve was also in obedience to the law (cf. Lk 2:41). Jesus himself obeyed Mary and Joseph in Nazareth (cf. Lk 2:51). During his public life, he paid tribute to Caesar and told people to do the same (cf. Mt 17:24–27; 22:16–22). At the unjust trial, Jesus recognized the authority of Pontius Pilate, although the latter was a coward and unjust (cf. Jn 18:28; 19:6). Such considerations will help the consecrated person to obey and trust in God's Providence.

Genuine religious obedience shows that there is no contradiction between obedience and freedom (cf. *Vita Consecrata*, 91). It is a shining example to society that people in positions of authority have to carry out their duties with a high sense of responsibility and service and that everyone has something to contribute to further harmony and the attainment of the goals of society.

VI

Community Life

The Second Vatican Council wisely observes that "God did not create man for life in isolation, but for the formation of social unity" (*Gaudium et Spes*, 32). "It has pleased God to make men holy and save them not merely as individuals, without any mutual bonds, but by making them into a single people, a people which acknowledges him in truth and serves him in holiness" (*Lumen Gentium*, 9). It is God, therefore, who gave human beings a social nature. They need interaction with other humans in order to reach, each of them, the height of their potential, in order to become all they can become, in order to develop fully their various talents.

Jesus gave his Church a communitarian character. He taught his followers to treat one another as brothers and sisters. He prayed that his followers be one, as he and the Father are one. He taught them to love others even to the point of sacrificing their life for them: "Greater love has no man than this, that a man lay down his life for his friends" (Jn 15:13). His Church is the new family of God.

Life in community is the usual form taken by the consecrated life, although hermits are also approved in Church life. Community life trains us in many virtues, including consideration for others, punctuality, the readiness to sacrifice one's personal choice for the sake of what others want or what the rule lays down, willingness to go to the place of work when one might have preferred to rest, and accepting and carrying out the work that one is given rather than the work of personal choice. Community life also includes acceptance of other people, with their faults and idiosyncrasies (and each one should not forget that he also has faults and idiosyncrasies). It can mean having to live for quite a number of years with a person one may not like and having to control one's desire to do things differently or to complain. A person who is alone may imagine that he is a saint, while indeed this may not be the case. The solitary may consider himself patient and considerate, whereas there is no proof because these virtues can be tested and proved only in interaction with other people. If a person is a good member of the community, if it is a joy for other people to live with that person, are these not signs that that person may well be on the road to sanctity?

A community is made up of many persons who have different characters, talents, and defects. Life in community demands a continued exercise of patience. It is not reasonable to expect that everything will evolve according to one's personal tastes and choices. Nor is it possible or wise always to correct what could be done better or differently. A member who sets out to correct every fault or defect, true or imagined, without the patience to wait for the most suitable time and to avoid insulting other people would not be a pleasant companion. On the other hand, when someone has tried to correct me, I should ask myself whether I humbly recognize my mistake and accept my fault or whether I rather invent a whole chain of explanations and excuses in an effort to cut a fine figure. It will do the members of a community some good if they reflect on the patience of Jesus our Master with the Pharisees and scribes who kept harassing him, with his Apostles, who were often slow to understand, or with Peter, who denied him in a moment of weakness, or with Pontius Pilate, who delivered an unjust judgment, or with Judas Iscariot, who betrayed a trust and would listen to no appeals.

In his meeting with the Union of Superiors General on November 29, 2013, Pope Francis was asked about fraternity in religious houses. The Holy Father answered that it has an enormous power of attraction. It presupposes the acceptance of differences and conflict. Sometimes it is hard to live, but if it is not lived, it does not bear fruit. In any case, "we must never manage in the conflict of a brother: we must treat the conflict with care" (*L'Osservatore romano*, weekly English ed., December 6, 2013, p. 7).

Every consecrated person should love his community. It is that person's spiritual home. It offers him a welcome, an approved way of life, the good example of other members, and the good will of the Church in the parish and the diocese. The community channels the zeal and love of the individual for God and neighbor. In sickness and old age, the member receives good care. At death he is given a decent burial and is guaranteed the prayers of the community. If a member did not love the community, would he not be behaving like a parasite?

Saint Augustine speaks to us in a moving way about love of neighbor. "Since you do not yet see God, you merit the vision of God by loving your neighbor. By loving your neighbor you prepare to see God. . . . Love your neighbor, then, and see within yourself the power by which you love your neighbor; there you will see God, as far as you are able. . . . In loving your neighbor and caring for him you are on a journey. . . . Support, then, this companion of your pilgrimage if you want to come into the presence of the one with whom you desire to remain for ever" (*Tract* 17, 7–9: CCL 36:174–75; Liturgy of the Hours, Office of Readings for Tuesday before Epiphany).

A temptation from which even consecrated persons cannot be exempted is that of rivalry, envy, and jealousy. Saint Basil the Great and Saint Gregory Nazianzen give us good example on this point. The Church celebrates both friends together on January 2. In the homily by Saint Gregory Nazianzen, we read: "The same hope inspired us: the pursuit of learning. This is an ambition especially subject to envy. Yet between us there was no envy. On the contrary, we made capital out of our rivalry. Our rivalry consisted, not in seeking the first place for oneself but in yielding it to the other, for we each looked on the other's success as his own" (*Oratio 43, in laudem Basilii Magni*, 20: PG 36:514–23; Liturgy of the Hours, Office of Readings for January 2). This is the sort of saintly example that builds up community life.

The Gospel tells us how the Lord Jesus himself handled a case of this temptation. John said to him: " 'Master, we saw a man casting out demons in your name, and we forbade him, because he does not follow with us.' But Jesus said to him, 'Do not forbid him; for he that is not against you is for you' " (Lk 9:49–50).

The early Church community had "one heart and soul" (Acts 4:32). Saint Paul exhorts the Galatians to carry one another's burdens (cf. Gal 6:2). A community of consecrated people should function as brothers or sisters gathered together in the Lord's name and rejoicing in his presence. It is Jesus himself who tells us that where two or three are gathered together in his name, there he is in their midst (cf. Mt 18:20).

Saint Paul exhorts the Ephesians to accept one another: "I therefore, a prisoner for the Lord, beg you to walk in a manner worthy of the calling to which you have been called, with all lowliness and meekness, with patience, forbearing one another in love, eager to maintain the unity of the Spirit in the bond of peace" (Eph 4:1–3). Saint Peter exhorts his Christians to "have unity of spirit, sympathy, love of the brethren, a tender heart and a humble mind" (1 Pet 3:8). These are precious ingredients for community life.

The Psalmist eulogizes life together in love: "Behold, how good and pleasant it is when brothers dwell in unity! It is like the precious oil upon the head, running down upon the beard, upon the beard of Aaron, running down on the collar of his robes! It is like the dew of Hermon, which falls on the mountains of Zion! For there the LORD has commanded the blessing, life for evermore" (Ps 133:1–3).

While every member of a consecrated community has a part to contribute, the role of the superior needs special mention. The superior should encourage, nourish, and sustain. He should find a way to encourage the strong to do even better and the weak not to despair. The prophet Isaiah says of the Messiah: "He will not cry or lift up his voice, or make it heard in the street; a bruised reed he will not break, and a dimly burning wick he will not quench" (Is 42:2–3). A superior should strive to be a little image of that. From the spirit of the founder of the consecrated family, and from the approved constitutions, rules, and customs, the superior will gather inspirations on how best to promote harmony, love, and growth in the community.

The Holy Eucharist is to be given a central place in each community. It is Jesus in this mystery of faith who calls the consecrated together, gives them life, and inspires them to open out to other people, especially the needy. "No Christian community", says the Second Vatican Council, can be "built up unless it has its basis and center in the celebration of the most Holy Eucharist; from this, therefore, all education to the spirit of community must take its origin. This celebration, if it is to be genuine and complete, should lead to various works of charity and mutual help, as well as to missionary activity and to different forms of Christian witness" (*Presbyterorum Ordinis*, 6). Although the Council is speaking in the context of the ministry of priests, which is often in parish communities, what it says here concerning the central place of the Holy Eucharist is fully applicable to communities of consecrated persons.

We should also add that a community of consecrated people should not be closed in upon itself. It should open out to the parish, the diocese, and the universal Church. It should show great interest in the missionary activity of the Church. And in a particular way it should do all it can to show Christian solidarity to the poor and the needy. Each community will study to see what it can do, taking into account its charism, its possibilities, and the area in which it is located. Pope Francis is for the whole Church a model for how to open out to those who are on the periphery of life.

Prophetic Dimension
of the Consecrated Life

In the Old Testament, God called the people of Is-
rael to be his own (cf. Exod 5:1–3). In the New
Testament, the people gathered together by Christ,
the Church, are the new family of God, consecrated,
covenanted. These people are to walk in the ways of
the Lord.

In the Old Testament, the prophets served, not
only to foretell the future, but also to alert people to
their duties regarding the covenant with God. They
kept reminding the chosen people of the importance
of the worship of the one true God, of obedience to
his commandments, of justice toward their neighbor, of love of the poor, and of the duty to offer
God true liturgical worship. They warned the people against the worship of alien gods, the adoption
of pagan customs, injustice toward one's neighbor,
and the oppression of the poor by those in authority. Elijah was a courageous prophet and friend of
God. He lived in God's presence. He defended the
worship of the true God against the pretenses of the

false prophets of Baal. He boldly announced God's will. He defended God's sovereignty. He came to the defense of the poor against the powerful of the world (cf. 1 Kings 18 and 19). He is a model of a consecrated person who lives the prophetic charism authentically.

In the New Testament, people in the consecrated state are called to be like leaven in society, to fulfill a prophetic role in radically calling the attention of society to the importance of following Christ. We are disciples of Christ. We are to take the Gospel call to discipleship seriously. The consecrated keep on reminding us of this fact, like the prophets of the Old Testament. The consecrated state has a prophetic dimension because it is a living eschatological sign. It reminds us of the world to come. Consecrated persons and their communities are called to be living witnesses of the kingdom of heaven by their lives of faith, hope, and charity. They point others in the Church, and even outside the Church, toward a communal future in union with the Blessed Trinity and the saints through their witness.

Life according to the three evangelical counsels of chastity, poverty, and obedience challenges the current of life in society. When authentically lived, "the decision to follow the counsels, far from involving an impoverishment of truly human values, leads instead to their transformation. The evangelical counsels should not be considered as a denial of the values inherent in sexuality, in the legitimate desire to possess material goods or to make decisions for oneself. . . . The profession of chastity, poverty and obedience is a warning not to underestimate the wound of original sin and, while affirming the value of created goods, *it relativizes them* by pointing to God as the absolute good. Thus, while those who follow the evangelical counsels seek holiness for themselves, they propose, so to speak, a spiritual 'therapy' for humanity, because they reject the idolatry of anything created and in a certain way they make visible the living God" (*Vita Consecrata*, 87).

If consecrated persons are to discharge well their prophetic role, heavy demands are made on them. They are to be people in union with God. Their lives have to shine with moral righteousness so that people who approach them go away convinced that they have been with a man or woman of God who derives strength from an inner force. They are to be genuine in such a way that their lives are in perfect accord with their words. Disinterestedness in material goods and things of this world should mark their life-style. Something of the austerity of Saint John the Baptist adds to their credibility. They are likely to attract admirers more by their life than by their verbal appeal for followers.

Saint John Paul II insists on the importance of consecrated people giving prophetic witness by the good example of their lives: "Prophecy derives a particularly persuasive power from *consistency between proclamation and life*. Consecrated persons will be faithful to their mission in the Church and the world, if they can renew themselves constantly in the light of the word of God. Thus will they be able to enrich the other faithful with the charismatic gifts they have received and, in turn, let themselves be challenged by the prophetic stimulus which comes from other sectors of the Church" (*Vita Consecrata*, 85).

Those who exercise a prophetic role should not be surprised if they meet with coldness or even opposition. They may not be easy to live with, because although they may concentrate on comforting the afflicted, they may unconsciously afflict the comfortable. People who live mediocre lives or who prefer to remain comfortable in their social nests may think the prophets upset the status quo and accuse them of being disturbers of the peace.

Social prophets can be seen as a threat by people in authority, especially if such people have some skeletons in their closet, if they have hidden faults, or if they are not entirely fair to their subjects. This can happen with respect to both religious and civil authorities. They can look on those who exercise the prophetic role as an embarrassment, or worse. The wicked king Ahab said to the prophet Elijah: "Have you found me, O my enemy?" The prophet answered: "I have found you, because you have sold yourself to do what is evil in the sight of the LORD" (1 Kings 21:20–21). Prophets are not safe in the hands of the high and mighty. Elijah received special help from God to escape the clutches of Ahab. As for Herod, he pretended to like to listen to John the Baptist, but he was uncomfortable with the call to justice and chastity by this great herald of Christ. He conveniently cut off his head to please Herodias and to pretend that he was being faithful to his sworn oath (cf. Mt 14:3–11). It is not, therefore, a surprise if some consecrated people living a prophetic life are ignored, disliked, marginalized, or even persecuted.

Authentic living of the three evangelical counsels goes against the current of life in the world and is therefore prophetic because it is countercultural. It is very demanding for the consecrated. "Prophetic witness requires the constant and passionate search for God's will, for self-giving, for unfailing communion in the Church, for the practice of spiritual discernment and love of the truth. It is also expressed through the denunciation of all that is contrary to the divine will and through the exploration of new ways to apply the Gospel in history, in expectation of the coming of God's Kingdom" (*Vita Consecrata*, 84).

It follows that if consecrated people do not live their calling authentically, they become a problem and an embarrassment for the Church. They begin to look like caricatures. Whereas if they are genuine in their consecrated state, they win credibility among the people. They plead for the poor and the marginalized, and people tend to give them what they ask for, because their lives are regarded as being in line with their request. They live what they preach. They reflect God, who is justice, love, and compassion. It is no wonder that religious leaders like Saint John Bosco and Blessed Mother Teresa of Calcutta were able to set up many works of charity for the poor and forgotten, with much support from the rich and the not so rich.

To say that consecrated people should be prophetic does not mean that they are out on purpose to oppose other members of the Church. But by their lives, and sometimes words, they can make others uncomfortable and give indications and suggestions about changes needed in Church structures and vocations in the world. Saint Francis of Assisi, although his life was highly prophetic at a time when there was corruption among some clerics, did not attack the bishops and the pope. The Saint of Assisi did not set out to reform the Church but, rather, to live the Gospel without compromise. He aimed at reforming himself. In this way, he and his companions contributed to the reform of the Church. Although the prophetic function and the hierarchical ministry in the Church do not coincide, they are both at the service of the Bride of Christ. The mystic Saint Catherine of Siena promoted peace and reconciliation between Italian towns, defended the rights and freedom of the Roman Pontiff, and played an important role in returning the papacy from Avignon to Rome in 1377. Although she herself was unschooled, her many letters and other works are prodigious, and in 1970 she was proclaimed, together with Saint Teresa of Avila, to be a doctor of the Church. She was prophetic! "Being prophets may sometimes imply making waves", says Pope Francis. "Prophecy makes noise, uproar, some say 'a mess'. But in reality, the charism of religious people is like yeast: prophecy announces the spirit of the Gospel" (interview in *America*, September 30, 2013, p. 28).

Moreover, consecrated people do not suggest that they have a monopoly on the prophetic role in Church or in society. God can manifest himself through anyone, cleric, religious, or lay person. His light on society can come sometimes through an unexpected channel.

VIII

Religious Institutes
of Brothers

Religious brothers and religious sisters take the same vows of chastity, poverty, and obedience. But because quite a number of people do not understand the vocation of the religious brothers, it will be useful to say a word about them here.

As mentioned earlier in this book, the consecrated life is by its nature neither lay nor clerical. Both clerics and laymen and women can become religious. The religious state as the "profession of the evangelical counsels is complete in itself. Consequently, both for the individual and for the Church, it is a value in itself, apart from the sacred ministry" (*Vita Consecrata*, 60). All religious, whether monks or nuns, brothers or sisters, take the same basic three vows. Religious institutes of brothers are congregations of men who live the three vows as brothers of Jesus Christ, brothers of one another, and brothers to everyone they serve.

Religious brothers are members of a variety of religious communities that may be contemplative, monastic, or apostolic (that is, of active works) in character. Some religious institutes are founded for brothers only. Some religious congregations for brothers can provide for a few brothers to be ordained priests. Monasteries generally have a good number of members who are both priests and monks along with all the other member monks. As monks, all of them are on an equal basis. Obviously, to function as a priest at Mass or in the confessional is reserved to the ordained monks. Some religious institutes of the active life are founded indeed for brothers, as remarked above, but can also provide for a few members to be ordained priests, often for the supply of the priestly ministry within the institute. There is therefore considerable variety in these institutes of the consecrated life.

As a religious brother or a monk, a person may be a teacher, professor, nurse, medical doctor, electrician, engineer, cook, lawyer, technician, artist, scientist, bookbinder, etc., according as the needs of his monastery or institute or the wider Church may indicate.

A religious brother is a mature man who feels called to the consecrated life, a life that closely imitates Jesus' way of life while on earth. The brother wants to follow Christ, who was chaste, poor, and obedient. He embraces this form of life in community, that is, in the company of like-minded brothers.

He is given formation and training in the apostolate that will enable him to exercise his gifts in the service of God's people. He accepts the cross of Jesus in his life and work and is happy and contented. He has not undertaken this way of life for any material advantage for himself or for his relatives. He is happy to be a friend of Jesus and a child of Mary. He calmly awaits his eternal reward.

The religious brother is aware that in the Church, bishops and priests are representatives of Christ as Head and Shepherd and as Spouse of the Church. Clerics are leaders and hierarchical ministers in the Church. The brother realizes that this is not his vocation. He just wants to follow Christ with a radical living of the Gospel. Therefore, the brother does not want people to mistake him for the priest or to be contrasted with him. He is not disappointed when he is not given the honors in society that some people associate with the priest.

The brother is also aware that many people do not understand him or his way of life. He is not angry if he receives humiliation from people who do not understand. He is happy that he has found the kingdom of heaven like a treasure and that he has sold all that he has to buy it (Mt 13:44). Jesus was aware that most of the people of Nazareth and elsewhere in the Holy Land did not know who he really was. The brother is calm when people do not know his identity. It is more important for the brother to have a clear image of his own identity and for him not to allow anyone to make him doubt his vocation. The Church absolutely needs men, and not only women, who will witness to Jesus in the radical and counter-cultural way in which genuine religious do.

When I asked people to describe the ideal brother in a religious institute of active life, they replied in the following terms: A brother is a man who is dedicated, committed, humble, and happy in his life of consecration to God. His life convinces people of the greatness of God and of the passing nature of the things of this world. He is near to the poor, the downtrodden, the dejected, the orphan, and the widow. He is a role model in training children in schools and catechism classes. He does not occupy a place of honor in church, and he shows people what genuine religion is all about. He is well educated, efficient in his special area, and a capable educator of young people. He diffuses calm and joy, and people are not afraid to approach him. In all these ways, he leads many people to God.

It is very encouraging that there are many people who appreciate the vocation of religious brothers. They see in them an inspiration to follow Jesus Christ and to strive to be detached from things of this world, each person according to his vocation. Some people who tend to be overawed by bishops or priests may feel more at ease with religious brothers.

I have seen this happen with locally founded brothers' congregations in areas of recent evangelization.

Why, then, do some people not understand the vocation of religious brothers? Why do they find it unattractive? In many social celebrations and even in homilies, priests and sisters receive due mention, but brothers are often forgotten. A brother who had studied philosophy and theology in Rome was asked by a priest why he was wasting his life as a brother instead of going the whole way and becoming a priest. Some parish priests want only one brother in the parish and do not see why there should be a community of two or three brothers, because they think of the brother primarily as an honest worker and not as a religious whose way of life calls for community living.

These observations should not be generalized to apply to all parts of the world or to all religious families of brothers. Worthy of special mention are religious brothers who are Benedictine or Cistercian monks or those who are Capuchin or Dominican friars. There are also many brothers in big religious congregations, like the Brothers of the Christian Schools, the Marist Brothers of the Schools, the Brothers of the Holy Cross, the Institute of the Brothers of the Christian Schools (also known as the De La Salle Brothers), the Brothers of Christian Instruction of Saint Gabriel (the Gabrielites), and the Congregation of Christian Brothers. These congregations of brothers have for centuries made their mark in Church life, service, and the education of children or even in the medical apostolate, like the Fatebenefratelli, who run the Saint Bartholomew Hospital in Rome. Church history has given such religious brothers a clear identity.

There are some clerical religious orders or institutes that, although founded for religious who will generally be ordained priests, also have room for some members who are brothers. Examples are the Society of Jesus, the Holy Ghost Congregation, and the Salesians. As members of such religious families, the brothers are on an equal status with the priest members. But since the vast majority of members are ordained priests, it is understandable that some may regard the members who are brothers as ranked below those who are priests.

A diocesan priest can also desire to become a religious, especially in a monastic community. For Nigerians, the first example is Blessed Cyprian Michael Iwene Tansi, O.C.S.O., who, after thirteen years as a diocesan priest, entered a Cistercian Abbey.

What is certain is that in some parts of the world, people tend to contrast the brother with the priest and to consider the brother inferior. They appreciate the priest because in Church celebrations he carries out a prominent role. He celebrates Mass, hears confessions, conducts marriages and funerals, preaches, and blesses. So people ask themselves why a brother, a mature man, does not go the whole way. Why should he stop halfway, since he has already entered Church ministry? Could it be that he did not do enough studies to qualify for the priesthood and possibly later for the episcopate?

People fail to consider that the religious brother takes the same vows as the religious sister and that therefore both are consecrated religious on an equal footing. Some reason that women cannot be ordained priests but that nothing is preventing a brother from going the whole way. This is not good theology. It manifests ignorance of the essence of the religious life.

It is necessary to understand the vocation of the priest and then that of the brother. The ministry of the priest is to celebrate the sacred mysteries, to preach the word of God, and to gather the people of God together under the leadership of the bishop. The vocation of the religious brother is the radical following of Christ by living the three evangelical counsels. The two vocations are different. The Church needs both. The two are not of the same species. The brother is not a minor edition of the priest!

Other people do not appreciate the brother sufficiently because they contrast him with the priest and they notice that the priest has a higher visibility in the Church, greater commanding authority, the capacity to have personal money and property and the ability to help his relatives financially (if he is a diocesan priest and not a religious priest). But the priesthood is not about having power and money and social status; rather, it is about spreading the Gospel and serving the people of God. Religion is about attention to God, union with God, knowledge of God, living for God, and having him as the absolute in one's life. Service of our neighbor is a necessary manifestation. Neither priests nor brothers nor sisters should be striving to acquire a high position or money through the Church. Jesus is our model. He makes a different appeal: "Whoever would be great among you must be your servant, and whoever would be first among you must be slave of all. For the Son of man also came not to be served but to serve, and to give his life as a ransom for many" (Mk 10:43–45).

Let us thank God for the vocation of the religious brothers and pray that it may be ever better understood, loved, lived, and supported in the Church and in society.

IX

Blessings That the Consecrated Life Brings to Church and Society

From the above considerations, one can see that the consecrated life brings many blessings to Church and society. Let us list some of them.

The consecrated life announces without words that nothing is too precious to offer to God. Some people do not understand, and they ask if it is not a " 'waste' of human energies which might be used more efficiently for a greater good, for the benefit of humanity and the Church" (*Vita Consecrata*, 104). They ask why monks and nuns spend many hours in singing the Divine Office in church and in silent contemplation. We answer with Saint John Paul II that such objections are "a consequence of a utilitarian and technocratic culture which is inclined to assess the importance of things and even of people in relation to their immediate 'usefulness' " (ibid.). We recall that Mary of Bethany poured a costly ointment of pure nard on the feet of Jesus (cf. Jn 12:3). What Mary did was an act of love that goes beyond all utilitarian considerations. "From such a life 'poured out' without reserve there spreads a fragrance which fills the whole house" (*Vita Consecrata*, 104).

Both Church and society need people and centers that elevate the human soul to God and remind everyone that the Creator should be the focus of our lives and endeavors. "In our world, where it often seems that the signs of God's presence have been lost from sight", says Saint John Paul II, "a convincing prophetic witness on the part of consecrated persons is increasingly necessary. In the first place this should entail *the affirmation of the primacy of God and of eternal life*, as evidenced in the following and imitation of the chaste, poor and obedient Christ who was completely consecrated to the glory of God and to the love of his brethren" (*Vita Consecrata*, 85).

Religious houses, and especially monasteries, are places of prayer, penance, silence, and quiet spiritual reflection. In the rush and hurry of life in the world, their role is important. There is also in many technologically developed societies a growing current of secularization, in which people live and work as if God did not exist. A monastery is an encouragement, without words, to avoid this aberration and also a proposal of what is possible, without offense to anyone.

Contemplatives in monasteries are carrying out an important service to mankind. These prophetic men and women are like sentinels. They are witnesses of hope that daylight is coming. They have put God at the center of their lives, and they carry in their hearts and in their prayer the joys and the hopes, the difficulties and sufferings of mankind. They thus show that they are at all times in profound communion with mankind. Led by the Holy Spirit, they strive to see people and events as God sees them (cf. José Rodriguez Carballo in *L'Osservatore romano*, November 30, 2013, p. 8). And each day, they offer prayers and sacrifices to beg God to have mercy on the world, to forgive men their offenses, and to give them that peace which they cannot give themselves. Those people are therefore mistaken who imagine that contemplatives are a waste or that they are irrelevant to the needs of this world.

The human heart is attracted by the desire to dominate, to be at the head, and to have power to command others and tell them what to do. This applies in both political and inner Church structures. The vows of obedience and poverty, when authentically lived, deliver a salutary message: readiness to serve, authority seen as service and not as domination, and readiness to contribute to harmony in society. This says something very useful to those politicians who regard political elections as a matter of life and death, to those candidates who find it difficult to accept election defeat and congratulate the winner, and also to those who get elected and then proceed to celebrate without moderation and who, once in office, seek occasions to reward their "friends" and punish their "enemies", forgetting that they were elected to serve all the people.

Showmanship and flamboyance by the high and mighty are temptations that many people in public life find difficult to resist. The consecrated life swims against their current. It encourages moderation, self-sacrifice, and acceptance of other people as brothers and sisters in the pilgrimage that is life on earth. No doubt, we cannot expect a political leader to copy exactly the self-effacing behavior of a Cistercian monk or the detachment from money of a Capuchin friar. But these religious can inspire the politician to put more Christian witness into his service in the political sphere. Moreover, religious institutes can demonstrate the proper exercise of democracy in the way they conduct elections: a religious who was for many years superior general just reverts to being an ordinary member of the institute when not reelected.

Dishonesty in the administration of public funds, embezzlement, and corrosive corruption have done much damage to many societies and have retarded development. Some people want to reap where they did not sow. They are not satisfied with their salaries. The common man who should receive from such people what is due to him cannot hope to get it unless he knows somebody, who knows somebody, who knows somebody. Granted, this is not the situation of public service in every country in the world. But it does happen in quite a number of countries. The vows of poverty and obedience authentically lived by consecrated people can encourage the lay faithful to be model Christians in politics and general administration. It is a happy thing that the causes of beatification of President Nyerere of Tanzania and of La Pira, Mayor of Florence, are being promoted.

Many societies suffer from various offenses against marriage and the family. Sexual relations outside marriage and the exploitation of people are sad realities, as the newspapers document. Consecrated people who live the vow of chastity are a silent witness that, with God's grace, self-control is possible and is a necessary road to maturity, self-respect, reverence for other people, and joy. If people would allow themselves to be inspired by such good examples, one source of suffering and tension in society could be removed.

In particular, the consecrated woman is a tribute to femininity, to humanity, and to the power of God's grace. When a girl enters the convent, some people may wonder whether she has had a sad or disappointing love relationship. No. It is the opposite. She is in love with God, who is love itself (cf. 1 Jn 4:16). She gives herself totally to God. The feminine soul has the characteristic, the power, to love, to give life, to look after life, and to defend life. A

genuine woman is mother, giving birth to natural
life or spiritual life. By special divine intervention,
the Blessed Virgin Mary combines virginity and ma-
ternity. She is "our tainted nature's solitary boast",
as the poet William Wordsworth has called her (in
his poem "The Virgin" in 1798, in *Ecclesiastical Son-
nets*). In a special way, she is a model of the consecrated woman. The dignity of women has often
been misunderstood, misinterpreted, maligned, and
offended. The consecrated woman helps to redeem
this treasure. She is also a mystical bride of Christ.
And the whole Church is the Spouse of Christ, from
whom she receives every good thing. "This spousal
dimension, which is part of all consecrated life, has
a particular meaning for women, who find therein
their feminine identity and as it were discover the
special genius of their relationship with the Lord"
(*Vita Consecrata*, 34).

Consecrated people help young people to learn the
proper attitude toward work and, in particular, to be
willing to work with their hands. Many young men
and women want to study, pass examinations, and get
a white-collar job. This is good. Society needs academicians and administrators. But a country should
also have technicians, electricians, radio and computer repairmen, cabinet workers, master builders,
engineers, vulcanizers, tailors, and farmers. Many of
these professions can also be studied even at the uni-

versity level. Universities should not be regarded as preparation for white-collar jobs alone. In monasteries, in particular, monks or nuns have traditionally done most of the work needed for the upkeep of the institution, including cultivation of the land. The Benedictine Monastery of Peramiho, for example, improved agricultural methods in a vast area of Tanzania and thus contributed much to the good of the area.

Parochialism, extreme ethnicism, and tribalism are obstacles on the road to national harmony in some countries. Religious congregations welcome candidates from many different backgrounds in terms of language and ethnic origins and teach them to accept one another and to learn to live and work as a religious family. The 1994 and 2008 World Synods of Bishops for Africa showed appreciation for the ability of religious congregations in Africa to contribute in this way an answer to tribalism. Pope Benedict XVI drew the attention of the Church in Africa to this witness of the consecrated life on the continent when he published his Post-Synodal Apostolic Exhortation *Africae Munus* in Cotonou on November 19, 2011. He declared: "Through the vows of chastity, poverty and obedience, the life of consecrated persons becomes a prophetic witness. Hence they can be examples in the area of reconciliation, justice and peace, even in circumstances marked by great tension. Community life shows us that it is possible to live as brothers and sisters, and to be united even when coming from different ethnic or racial backgrounds (cf. Ps 133:1). It can and must enable people to see and believe that today in Africa, those men and women who follow Christ Jesus find in him the secret of living happily together: mutual love and fraternal communion, strengthened daily by the Eucharist and the Liturgy of the Hours" (*Africae Munus*, 117).

Planning, execution, and continuity are needed if projects are to arise, continue, and last. Think of the building and running of a school, a college, a hospital, or a center for social assistance of disadvantaged citizens. While individuals can generate funds and start such projects, religious congregations offer greater assurance of continuity. They bring with them corporate responsibility. They have a continued supply of personnel. And their members have a sense of history and tradition that helps them respect the patrimony of their predecessors. History has proved that this is the case, considering the educational, medical, and social institutions that owe their origin and life to consecrated people or religious orders or congregations.

It is the religious motivation that helps to explain the immense devotion of religious sisters in the educational, medical, and social assistance fields all through the centuries. On the Day for Consecrated Life, on February 2, 2014, Pope Francis in his Angelus Message drew attention to how much Church and society owe to religious sisters. "Let us think a little", he said, "about what would happen if there were no sisters in hospitals, no sisters in missions, no sisters in schools. Think about a Church without sisters! It is unthinkable: they are this gift, this leaven that carries forward the People of God. These women who consecrate their life to God, who carry forward Jesus' message, are great. The Church and the world need this testimony of the love and mercy of God. The consecrated, men and women religious, are the testimony that God is good and merciful. . . . Prayer is needed so that many young people may answer 'yes' to the Lord who is calling them to consecrate themselves totally to him for selfless service to their brothers and sisters" (Angelus Message, in *L'Osservatore romano*, February 3–4, 2014, p. 8).

Clericalism can become a problem in the Church. Bishops and priests can imperceptibly take on more and more decision making in the Church, begin to see their role more as an exercise of power than as service, and not appreciate sufficiently the roles of lay people and religious. The love of titles can also threaten to become immoderate. A consecrated person who lives a humble and not overly prominent life can be a good tonic to clericalism. In the Church,

Jesus Christ is the center. Human beings are not the center of attention.

Sustained fidelity to promises made and constancy in one's vocation are needed in various walks of life. More and more people are finding it difficult to be bound for their whole lives by vows made at one milestone in their earthly pilgrimage. There are married people who after some years are tempted to want a change of partners. There are some candidates for the priesthood who would like to suggest that they serve as priests for a period of about ten years and thereafter be free to make a change of vocation. The constancy required in living the vows of the consecrated life with generosity until death is a good example of what fidelity and constancy should mean. With the help of God's sustaining grace, consecrated people prove, without words, that it is possible to remain faithful to vows pronounced until death. When a perpetually professed religious abandons the religious life, there is surprise.

The consecrated life is a general encouragement and promotion of religion as worship of God, service of God, and service of the neighbor, especially the poor and the needy. It is saying that life according to the Gospel is possible. Pope Benedict XVI said to religious superiors general: "The Gospel lived daily provides the element that gives fascination and beauty to the consecrated life and presents you to the world as a reliable alternative" (Address to the International Union of Superiors General, November 26, 2010).

We can conclude this listing of the blessings that the consecrated life can bring by saying with Saint John Paul II: "Look at these people seized by Christ, who show that in self-mastery, sustained by grace and God's love, lies the remedy for the craving to possess, to seek pleasure, to dominate. . . . Does not this world of ours need joyful witnesses and prophets of the beneficent power of God's love?" (*Vita Consecrata*, 108).

X

Challenges in
the Consecrated Life

In all states of life, there are some people who begin but who later, for one reason or another, do not persevere in that state of life, leaving it for another. It may or may not be their fault. I have been able to discuss with many consecrated people why this phenomenon is also found among them, what the causes might be, and what the remedies could be. An analysis of such situations can often suggest what might be done to promote a higher percentage of perseverance. It is therefore useful to survey some of the reasons why some consecrated people abandon their vocation. What challenges do they face?

One major problem is an insufficient life of union with God. This can be manifested by a poor life of prayer and sacramental participation, especially with reference to Penance and the Holy Eucharist. When the virtues of faith, hope, and charity are not strongly rooted in a person, the spiritual strength is not there to withstand the force of storms in later life. Sometimes there is too much concentration on apostolic works but not enough on the God of those works.

Allied to this is a lack of clarity on the part of the consecrated person about the correct placement of values: God, witnessing, fame, power, friends, family, or money. It is important that the person have clear priorities about who or what is his center of interest. Saint Paul tells his disciple Timothy: "I know whom I have believed, and I am sure that he is able to guard until that Day what has been entrusted to me" (2 Tim 1:12). To the Corinthians, Saint Paul writes about his clarity of spiritual vision and his conscious and disciplined living for the Gospel: "I do not run aimlessly, I do not box as one beating the air: but I pommel my body and subdue it, lest after preaching to others I myself should be disqualified" (1 Cor 9:26–27). If the consecrated person does not have robust faith, he can arrive at such a crisis that doubts begin about the Church herself or about the evangelical counsels and life according to them.

Inadequate involvement in the community dimension of the consecrated state is another negative indication. The sense of belonging to an order or religious congregation or other consecrated community can become more and more superficial. Disaffection can show itself in hypercriticism of the superiors or of the entire community. Stress in relationships with other members of the community can lead to growing disregard for community activities and more and more absenteeism by the member in crisis. Not loving to join the other members of the community at prayer, at table, and at recreation can gradually make a member look on the religious house as a hostel or simple residence. The situation can get worse if there are scandals, injustice, favoritism, or hypocrisy on the part of superiors or older members of the religious institute, or even only credible perceptions of such faults.

Problems and challenges regarding the vow of chastity need to be faced and resolved with honesty, generosity, and consultation with a clearheaded and God-fearing spiritual director. Even a reasonably good religious can unexpectedly fall in love with a particular individual. What is needed is to know how to handle such a situation with calm, promptness, and spiritual wisdom. Otherwise, there can be little compromises, if not downright infidelities, which indicate that the individual is now on a slippery slope.

There should be no market-value mentality regarding the consecrated state. What such people can produce is important. But of greater importance is the fact that they are consecrated. Every member of any particular community cannot be gifted with the highest degree of productivity as an academician, an engineer, an agriculturist, and so on. The community should have place for a member who is not particularly talented. No matter how poorly gifted, everyone is good at something, if only that particular area can be discovered and encouraged. Here it needs also to be stressed that the community should have a place for highly talented members. It can happen that such persons are marginalized or even oppressed and regarded as proud or ambitious. Petty jealousies can creep in. An institute of the consecrated life should rejoice to have gifted academicians or other superstars as members. And superiors should be careful not to surround themselves with mediocre members who never challenge any idea they propose for consideration. Wise and humble superiors know that they should not be afraid to listen to and accept ideas better than their own.

Initiation into the consecrated life should be built on firm foundations. Fear of the married state and its responsibilities, failure in a marriage proposal, the strong desire of parents to have a son or daughter consecrated, or the lack of attraction to a definite lay profession are not good reasons for entering the consecrated state and will not be able to sustain a person for life.

A young girl may have an idealized image of the religious life as a perfect life in which one finds harmony and holiness in every convent. If such a young person enters the convent and later also sees, along with holy sisters, members who envy and discriminate against others, she could become disillusioned and decide to leave. She was not trained to appreciate that not all members reach the spiritual heights that are expected of them.

Some people are by their personality not really suited to religious life. Even with all the honest efforts that such a person may make, community life may continue to be difficult, the vows extraordinarily difficult to observe, and relationships with other members often tense. These may be indications that the individual in question has another vocation, not that of consecration in that particular community.

Thought should also be given to those who embrace the consecrated life with zeal, joy, and all the good qualities to be desired for their state, but who later experience a series of tragedies, deaths in their biological families, chronic illnesses, and other grave misfortunes. The institute should with compassion be near such members to discern God's will for them.

More careful discernment during the early days of a postulant or novice should lead superiors to identify those candidates who have no real religious vocation. Such are those who, even unconsciously, use the consecrated state for self-promotion, prestige, opportunity for higher studies, social promotion, or the good name for the biological family.

Formation has great importance in the consecrated state. Initial formation in the postulancy and novitiate should be followed up with ongoing formation all through life. According to the talents of each person and obligations due to work assignments, all consecrated people should make progress in reading and discussing Church documents on the consecrated life. Attention to Holy Scripture and sacred theology as well as updating in assigned professional work have their importance, so that the consecrated person does not settle into a plateau of spiritual mediocrity.

In some cultures there is a growing belief that nobody should be permanently bound to one profession, one way of life, one promise made. If a consecrated person begins to absorb this virus, he will feel that the vows should not bind until death. This calls for serious reflection and prayer so that the consecrated person may see the truth with greater clarity. The Lord Jesus has told us: "No one who puts his hand to the plow and looks back is fit for the kingdom of God" (Lk 9:62).

It is not difficult to see that individualism, subjectivism, and selfishness do not promote the consecrated life. The attraction of the material goods of this world is always a challenge. It can be resisted. Unhealthy competition with other consecrated people or with the laity may be a temptation. But it can be resisted and need not be allowed to overcome a person.

The members of the biological family of the consecrated person can sometimes become part of the problem instead of being of support. If they begin to pressure their consecrated relative to channel Church or congregation money to them or if they interfere with superiors in suggesting where their relative should be assigned work, then they are pulling down instead of building up. It is true that situations vary around the world. There are consecrated people who come from rather rich families and who do not have the problem of maintenance for their relatives. Discernment and compassion are needed in all cases.

All the faults need not be on the side of the consecrated member who now feels obliged to look for another vocation. Superiors may also have a share in the setback. Superiors can ask themselves if they have shown sufficient wisdom and discernment in helping a candidate from the early days of his novitiate. Are the talents and capacities of the various candidates studied, appreciated, and taken into consideration in the assignment of work? Were superiors gentle enough with the weak and patient in encouraging him to improve, or, rather, did they break the bruised reed or quench the dimly burning wick (cf. Is 42:3)? Did superiors show partiality toward some candidates or lack the courage to send away an unsuitable candidate because the latter had a relative highly placed in Church or society or parents who donated generously to the religious congregation? As can be seen, it is not easy to be a superior.

This listing of some of the challenges to the conse-crated life also suggests what can be done. In sum-mary, it is essential that God be at the center of the life of each consecrated person. Initial and ongoing formation should focus on this. Community life is to be greatly encouraged. The radical nature of disciple-ship that the consecrated life demands should always be put before the candidates from the earliest days in the postulancy and novitiate. The choice of for-mation personnel assumes great importance. And it should always be remembered that while the main-tenance of works is necessary in each religious or other consecrated community, compassionate atten-tion to the state, spiritual and human growth, and performance of each of the members has a higher priority. Finally, each community, when it has done what it can, is to leave its present and its future in the invisible hands of Divine Providence.

XI

Responsibilities of the Church toward the Consecrated Life

Everyone in the Church has a role to play in the promotion of the consecrated life.

The first requirement is that the consecrated state be known. One cannot love and esteem what one does not understand. The role of priests and bishops in this information service is very important. It is they who preach to the people. It is they who are spiritual directors to help people discern their vocations. Therefore, the theology and canon law pertaining to the consecrated life should be carefully taught in seminaries and should receive continued attention in seminars for ongoing formation of priests. It is not to be presumed that every priest understands. Experience has shown that many priests do not understand the vocation to the state we are discussing.

On religious and social occasions, people should not forget religious brothers. Their witness and presence are important for the life of the Church. People should be shown that it is a mistake to consider brothers of less worth than priests.

Those who preach priestly and religious vocations have a big responsibility. Homilies should have theological and scriptural solidity, show the beauty of the consecrated life, and include all the various vocations in the Church, not forgetting religious brothers and members of secular institutes as well as consecrated virgins. The Second Vatican Council is rather insistent: "Priests and Christian educators should make serious efforts to foster religious vocations, thereby increasing the strength of the Church, corresponding to its needs. These candidates should be suitably and carefully chosen. In ordinary preaching, the life of the evangelical counsels and the religious state should be treated more frequently. Parents, too, should nurture and protect religious vocations in their children by instilling Christian virtue in their hearts" (*Perfectae Caritatis*, 24). Saint John Paul II speaks of the superiority of the consecrated state: "The whole Church finds in her hands this great gift and gratefully devotes herself to promoting it with respect, with prayer, and with the explicit invitation to accept it. It is important that Bishops, priests and deacons, convinced of the evangelical superiority of this kind of life, should strive to discover and encourage the seeds of vocation through preaching, discernment and wise spiritual guidance" (*Vita Consecrata*, 105).

Consecrated people are to be encouraged and supported in such ways as provision of land for their houses and projects, professional help from lawyers and architects, donation of money and goods, advice, and other signs of appreciation and esteem. The spiritual ministration offered by priests is underlined by the Second Vatican Council: "Priests should remember that all religious, both men and women, who certainly have a distinguished place indeed in the house of the Lord, deserve special care in their spiritual progress for the good of the whole Church" (*Presbyterorum Ordinis*, 6). Here is the place to pay tribute to those priests who for years make themselves available to consecrated people for Holy Mass, for the Sacrament of Penance, for spiritual retreats, and for funerals.

It is easy for priests and bishops to forget secular institutes and consecrated virgins in their preaching about vocations. And yet, these are also vocations that manifest a radical following of Jesus. Pastoral wisdom will indicate how best to introduce these ways of life.

Relatives are right to expect their children or brothers or sisters who are consecrated to pray for their biological family, visit them when possible, give them spiritual advice, contact them by telephone or email according to local possibilities, and be edifying by their lives of witness. Her relatives said to one professed sister: "Live your new life well. Do not disgrace us. You chose this life. Nobody forced you to it." Relatives are not to expect money from their member who is now a religious. They are not to pressure religious superiors to post their relative to places of their choice. And they are not to expect privileges in employment opportunities. The members of the biological family of someone in the early stages of religious formation will understandably expect many contacts, visits, telephone calls, and emails. With the passage of time, however, both sides must learn that this is one of the sacrifices to be made. The consecrated religious is called to be more and more focused on the new religious family or congregation and its apostolate and less on the biological family from which he came. Gradually, relatives will realize that it is not only their professed member who should make sacrifices; they themselves are also called to carry the cross, big or small, as it may be. Here it is proper to express gratitude to those families who have offered their sons or daughters to the consecrated life. May God bless them all with joy, peace, and grace.

It can also be added that institutes of the consecrated life should not always expect to be at the receiving end. Sometimes they have some of the best material things! The temptation to group selfishness can be real. Religious congregations and other institutes of the consecrated life are to be encouraged to give from the little they have, especially to the poor.

The widow's mite did not come from abundance. The widow "out of her poverty put in all the living that she had" (Lk 21:4).

Religious orders and congregations and secular institutes are to set great value on the formation of their members in matters spiritual, intellectual, communal, and apostolic. Frank and open dialogue on the various aspects of the consecrated life is necessary. "Formation is craftsmanship not enforcement", said Pope Francis, "and the goal is to train religious who have a heart that is tender, not sour like vinegar. We are all sinners, but we are not corrupt. We accept sinners, but not the corrupt" (Papal address to Union of Major Superiors, in *L'Osservatore romano*, weekly English ed., December 6, 2013, p. 7). Ongoing formation should deal with such issues as the challenges of human nature, mid-life crises, the possibility of loneliness, frustration, fear, and expressions of love that may not have been sufficiently covered during the initial formation in the novitiate. It is impressive that the *Code of Canon Law* dedicates three canons to formation (cann. 659–61).

The best preacher of the consecrated life is the consecrated person, brother or sister, monk or nun, member of secular institute or consecrated virgin, who is calm, holy, happy, efficient, and marked by psychological balance. Such a person is a spiritual magnet.

The Church dedicates the Feast of the Presentation of Our Lord on February 2 as the annual World Day for Consecrated Life, and the Memorial of the Presentation of the Blessed Virgin Mary, on November 21, as the annual day of prayer for those in monastic life. And now the year 2015 has been declared by Pope Francis as the Year for Consecrated Life. Consecrated people spontaneously and rightly look up to Our Blessed Mother as a model and pray for her intercession and protection.

Blessed be God, who in the wonders of his Providence has called many men and women to follow Christ with radical dedication in the consecrated life. To Jesus Christ, the mystical Spouse of the Church and the mystical Spouse of every consecrated person, be honor and glory. To the Holy Spirit, who, with the Father and the Son, is adored and glorified, be praise and thanksgiving for the grace of the consecrated life in the Church.

Abbreviations

ANF: *Ante-Nicene Fathers: The Writings of the Fathers Down to A.D. 325.* Edited by Alexander Roberts and James Donaldson. Revised by A. Cleveland Coxe, 10 vols. Peabody, Mass.: Hendrickson Pub., 1995.

CIC: Code of Canon Law. Translation prepared under the auspices of the Canon Law Society of America. Washington, D.C.: Canon Law Society of America, 1983.

NPNF, 1st series: *Nicene and Post-Nicene Fathers: A Select Library of the Christian Church.* First series. Edited by Philip Schaff. 14 vols. Peabody, Mass.: Hendrickson Pub., 1995.

NPNF, 2nd series: *Nicene and Post-Nicene Fathers: A Select Library of the Christian Church.* Second series. Edited by Philip Schaff and Henry Wace. 14 vols. Peabody, Mass.: Hendrickson Pub., 1995.